SCHOLASTIC

Arshia's

Cursive
Practice
Learning Pad

Dear Parents,

Welcome to the Scholastic Early Learners Cursive Practice Learning Pad.

The ability to write quickly and neatly benefits children, especially as they move higher in the education system. This learning pad will help ensure that children form cursive letters correctly right from the start. Regular practice builds up muscle memory, eventually allowing the writer to form words automatically, while focusing instead on the content of what they want to write.

Here are some tips to help ensure children get the most from these activities.

★ Encourage children to sit with their feet flat on the floor and their backs straight.

★ If possible, provide your child with a pencil to assist with forming smooth lines. Rollerball pens also write smoothly, but the marks cannot always be erased. Triangular shaped pencils and pens can help with grip.

★ Explain that when writing a word, the flicks on the letters should join up to form one continuous, flowing shape.

★ Help children understand the diagrams that show how to form the letters, particularly noting the order in which to follow the arrows. They can practice by drawing letters with a finger in the air, in sand, or on a flat surface.

★ Ensure children understand that the red hand symbol indicates when to lift the pencil off the page. Also, make sure they know not to dot an i or cross a t until they have finished writing the whole word.

★ Plan short, regular sessions only doing one or two pages at a time. Make the learning sessions enjoyable. Praise effort and improvement. For example, say: "You're working hard and so your letters are getting neater and neater."

We wish your child hours of enjoyment with this fun learning pad!

Scholastic Early Learners

The Position of the Page: To write on an even slant, angle the page at about 45 degrees or whatever feels most comfortable. For right-handers, the right side of the page should be higher; for left-handers the right side of the page should be lower.

Left-handed writing	**Right-handed writing**

The Letter **A**

Trace the **A** with your finger.

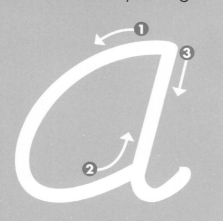

Trace the **A's**, and then write some A's of your own.

Trace the **a** with your finger.

Trace the **a's**, and then write some a's of your own.

Trace the words.

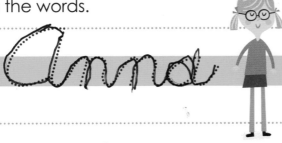

3

Trace the **B** with your finger.

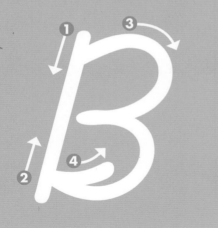

Trace the **B's**, and then write some B's of your own.

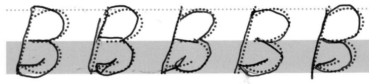

Trace the **b** with your finger.

Trace the **b's**, and then write some b's of your own.

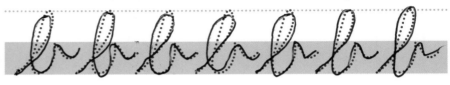

Trace the words.

Ben   *Bella*

bird   *bicycle*

ball

The Letter C

Trace the **C** with your finger.

Trace the **C's**, and then write some C's of your own.

Trace the **c** with your finger.

Trace the **c's**, and then write some c's of your own.

Trace the words.

Chloe   *Caden*

clock   *chair*

cat

Trace the **D** with your finger.

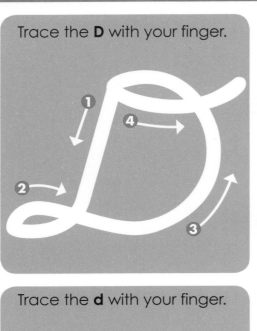

Trace the **D's**, and then write some D's of your own.

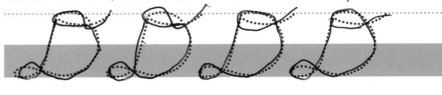

Trace the **d** with your finger.

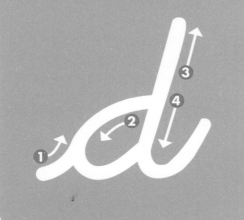

Trace the **d's**, and then write some d's of your own.

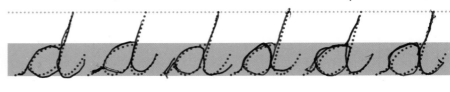

Trace the words.

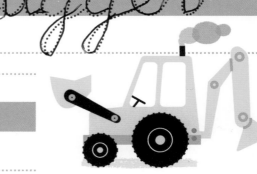

Trace the **E** with your finger.

Trace the **E's**, and then write some E's of your own.

Trace the **e** with your finger.

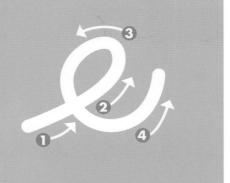

Trace the **e's**, and then write some e's of your own.

Trace the words.

Ethan

Ellie

emu

engine

eagle

Trace the **F** with your finger.

Trace the **F's**, and then write some F's of your own.

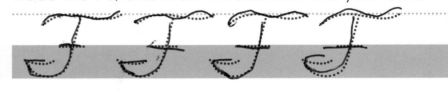

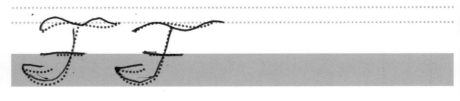

Trace the **f** with your finger.

Trace the **f's**, and then write some f's of your own.

Trace the words.

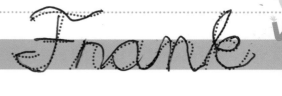

Trace the **G** with your finger.

Trace the **G's**, and then write some G's of your own.

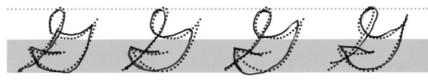

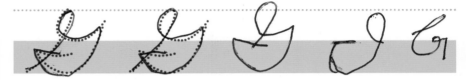

Trace the **g** with your finger.

Trace the **g's**, and then write some g's of your own.

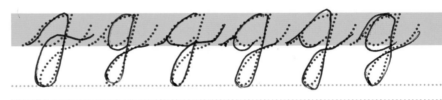

Trace the words.

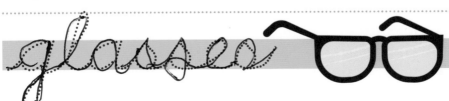

George   Grace

grapes   goat

glasses

Trace the **H** with your finger.

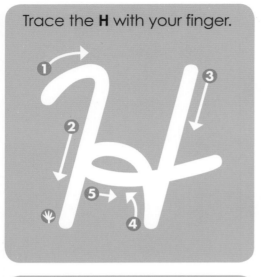

Trace the **H's**, and then write some H's of your own.

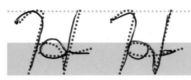

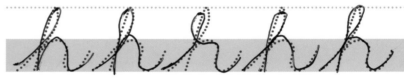

Trace the **h** with your finger.

Trace the **h's**, and then write some h's of your own.

Trace the words.

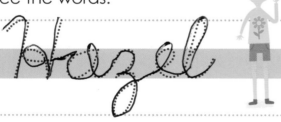

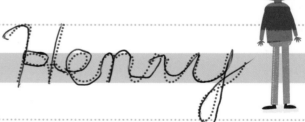

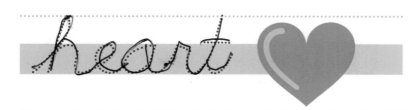

The Letter I

Trace the **I** with your finger.

Trace the **I's**, and then write some I's of your own.

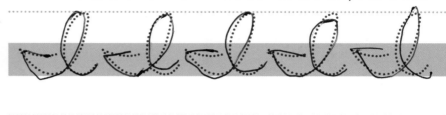

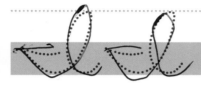

Trace the **i** with your finger.

Trace the **i's**, and then write some i's of your own.

Trace the words.

Ivan

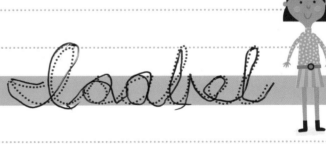

Isabel

insect

igloo

infant

The Letter J

Trace the **J** with your finger.

Trace the **J's**, and then write some J's of your own.

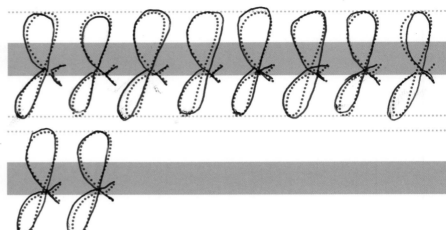

Trace the **j** with your finger.

Trace the **j's**, and then write some j's of your own.

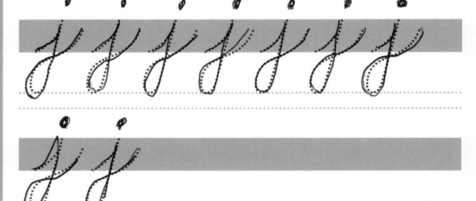

Trace the words.

Jack

Jada

jeans

jaguar

jewels

The Letter K

Trace the **K** with your finger.

Trace the **K's**, and then write some K's of your own.

Trace the **k** with your finger.

Trace the **k's**, and then write some k's of your own.

Trace the words.

Karl   Katie

koala   kayak

kitten

Trace the **L** with your finger.

Trace the **L's**, and then write some L's of your own.

Trace the **l** with your finger.

Trace the **l's**, and then write some l's of your own.

Trace the words.

Luke

Lily

lamp

lion

leaf

The Letter M

Trace the **M** with your finger.

Trace the **M's**, and then write some M's of your own.

Trace the **m** with your finger.

Trace the **m's**, and then write some m's of your own.

Trace the words.

Mateo   Mia

mouse   magnet

mermaid

15

The Letter **N**

Trace the **N** with your finger.

Trace the **N's**, and then write some N's of your own.

Trace the **n** with your finger.

Trace the **n's**, and then write some n's of your own.

Trace the words.

Nora

Noah

needle

nurse

nest

Trace the **O** with your finger.

Trace the **O's**, and then write some O's of your own.

Trace the **o** with your finger.

Trace the **o's**, and then write some o's of your own.

Trace the words.

Owen   Olivia

octopus   owl

orange

Trace the P with your finger.

Trace the P's, and then write some P's of your own.

PPPPPPP

PP

Trace the p with your finger.

Trace the p's, and then write some p's of your own.

p p p p p p p

p p

Trace the words.

Piper   Parker

pencil   puppy

parrot

Trace the **Q** with your finger.

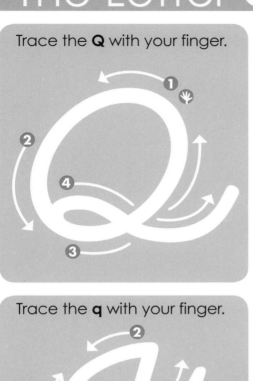

Trace the **Q's**, and then write some Q's of your own.

Trace the **q** with your finger.

Trace the **q's**, and then write some q's of your own.

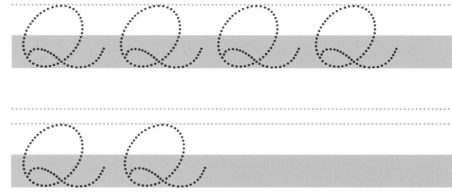

Trace the words.

Quentin   Quinn

quail   queen

question

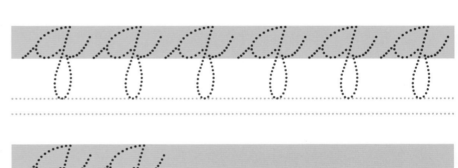

Trace the **R** with your finger.

Trace the **R's**, and then write some R's of your own.

Trace the **r** with your finger.

Trace the **r's**, and then write some r's of your own.

Trace the words.

Trace the **S** with your finger.

Trace the **S's**, and then write some S's of your own.

Trace the **s** with your finger.

Trace the **s's**, and then write some s's of your own.

Trace the words.

Sam   Sophia

spider   skates

shell

Trace the **T** with your finger.

Trace the **T's**, and then write some T's of your own.

Trace the **t** with your finger.

Trace the **t's**, and then write some t's of your own.

Trace the words.

The Letter U

Trace the **U** with your finger.

Trace the **U's**, and then write some U's of your own.

Trace the **u** with your finger.

Trace the **u's**, and then write some u's of your own.

Trace the words.

Usher   Una

ukulele   unicorn

uniform

The Letter V

Trace the **V** with your finger.

Trace the **V's**, and then write some V's of your own.

Trace the **v** with your finger.

Trace the **v's**, and then write some v's of your own.

Trace the words.

Victor   Vicky

vase   volcano

violin

Trace the **W** with your finger.

Trace the **W's**, and then write some W's of your own.

Trace the **w** with your finger.

Trace the **w's**, and then write some w's of your own.

Trace the words.

Will Wanda

watch wolf

wheel

Trace the **X** with your finger.

Trace the **X's**, and then write some X's of your own.

Trace the **x** with your finger.

Trace the **x's**, and then write some x's of your own.

Trace the words.

Xavier Xena

xylophone

X-ray

Trace the **Y** with your finger.

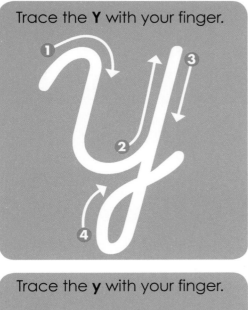

Trace the **Y**'s, and then write some Y's of your own.

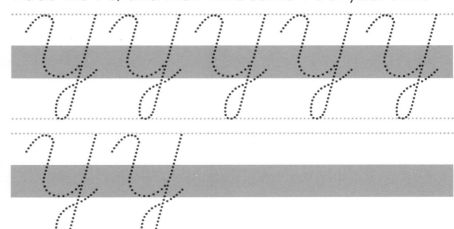

Trace the **y** with your finger.

Trace the **y**'s, and then write some y's of your own.

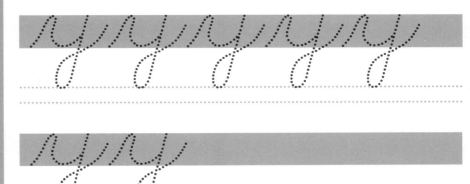

Trace the words.

The Letter Z

Trace the **Z** with your finger.

Trace the **Z's**, and then write some Z's of your own.

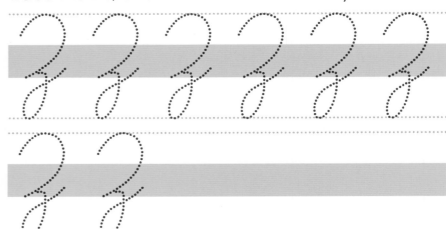

Trace the **z** with your finger.

Trace the **z's**, and then write some z's of your own.

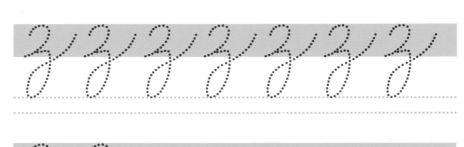

Trace the words.

Zack

Zita

zero

zigzag

zebra

Trace the numbers, and then write some of your own.

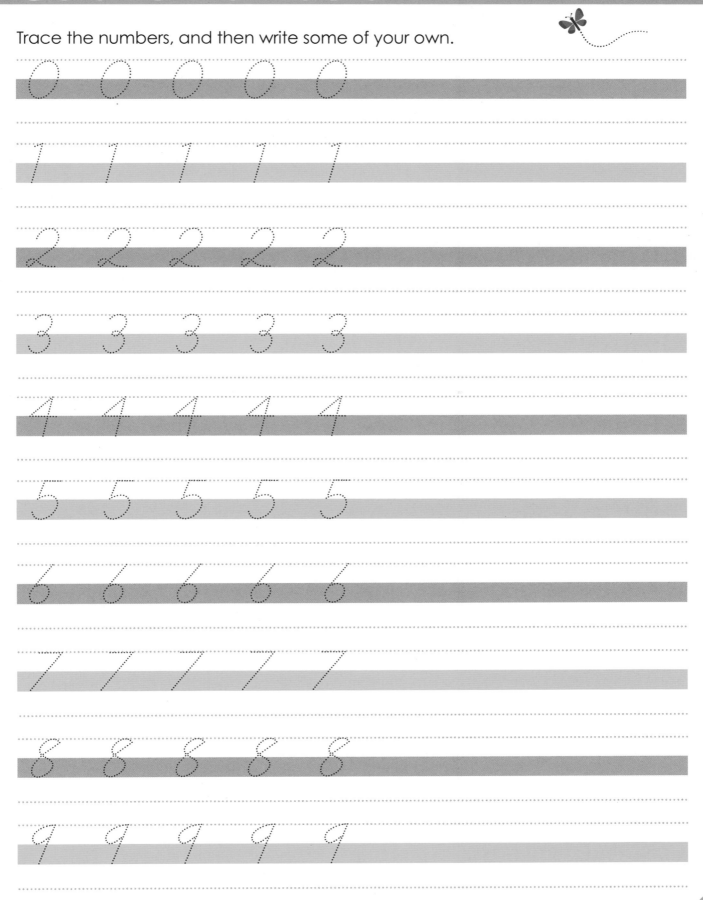

Many cursive letters join up, so you don't have to lift your pen as often. Finish the whole word before you add the dot above an **i** or the crossbar over a **t**.

Trace and write some joined **a's** and **d's**.

aaaa

dddd

Trace and write these words to practice joining **a's** and **d's**.

ant

bag

dog

duck

hedge

Trace and write some joined **h's** and **k's**.

hhhhh

kkkkkk

Trace and write these words to practice joining **h's** and **k's**.

hat

shed

key

kid

kick

Trace and write some joined **l's** and **t's**.

llll

tttt

Trace and write these words to practice joining **l's** and **t's**.

lamp

clip

tire

toad

star

Trace and write some joined **m's** and **n's**.

mmmm

nnnn

Trace and write these words to practice joining **m's** and **n's**.

lime

mug

man

pony

net

Trace and write some joined **c's** and **e's**.

ccccc

eeeee

Trace and write these words to practice joining **c's** and **e's**.

cat

lock

egg

eel

legs

Trace and write some joined **i's** and **j's**.

iiiii

jjjjj

Trace and write these words to practice joining **i's** and **j's**.

ice

fish

jam

jet

ajar

Trace and write some joined **b**'s and **o**'s.

bbbbb

ooooo

Trace and write these words to practice joining **b**'s and **o**'s.

bat

baby

old

off

frog

Trace and write some joined **f's** and **g's**.

ffffff

ggggg

Trace and write these words to practice joining **f's** and **g's**.

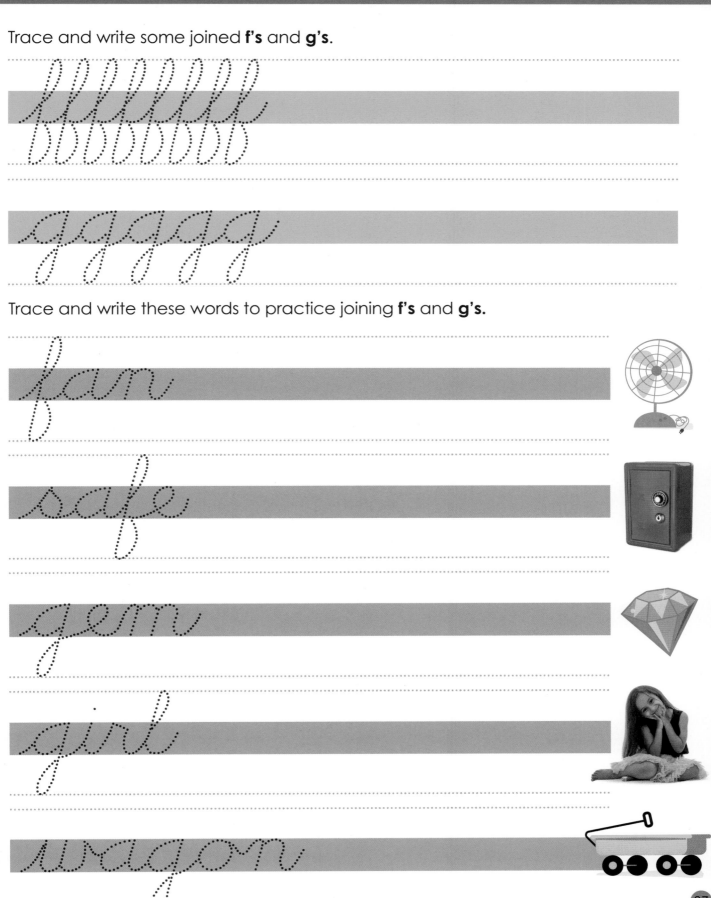

fan

safe

gem

girl

wagon

Trace and write some joined **p's** and **q's**.

ppppp

qqqqqq

Trace and write these words to practice joining **p's** and **q's**.

pet

skip

quill

quilt

square

Trace and write some joined **r's** and **s's**.

nnnnn

sssss

Trace and write these words to practice joining **r's** and **s's**.

run

grip

sloth

sob

nose

Trace and write some joined **u's** and **w's**.

uuuuuuuu

wwwwwww

Trace and write these words to practice joining **u's** and **w's**.

up

bus

watch

whale

fawn

Joining **v** and **x**

Trace and write some joined **v's** and **x's**.

Trace and write these words to practice joining **v's** and **x's**.

vet

wave

box

taxi

exit

EXIT

Trace and write some joined **y's** and **z's**.

yyyyyy

zzzzzzz

Trace and write these words to practice joining **y's** and **z's.**

yo-yo

hyena

zoo

zipper

buzz

Some uppercase letters don't join to other letters.
Trace and write these words with uppercase letters.

Blue

Dance

Flip

Owl

Pear

Shark

Team

Wolf

Some uppercase letters do join to other letters.
Trace and write these words with uppercase letters.

Acorn

Ape

Castle

Clam

Elf

Happy

Hug

Idea

44

Some uppercase letters do join to other letters.
Trace and write these words with uppercase letters.

Ink

Jay

Jump

Kite

Loop

Mask

Neat

Ninja

Some uppercase letters do join to other letters.
Trace and write these words with uppercase letters.

Quest

Read

Relay

Upset

Yak

Yawn

Year

Zebra

2021

Trace and write these sentences.

Otters sleep holding hands.

Ostriches lay the biggest eggs.

Write a sentence using one or more of these words.
Start with a capital letter, and end with a period.

otter   ostrich   sleep   biggest

Trace and write these sentences.

Jellyfish don't have brains.

A group of rats is a mischief.

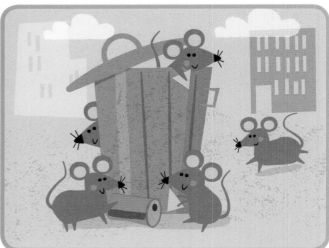

Write a sentence using one or more of these words.
Start with a capital letter, and end with a period.

brain   jellyfish   rat   mischief

Trace and write these sentences.

Bananas can be red or purple.

Hippos run faster than people.

Write a sentence using one or more of these words.
Start with a capital letter, and end with a period.

banana people purple hippo

Trace and write these sentences.

A corn kernel is a type of seed.

A tomato is a type of fruit.

Write a sentence using one or more of these words.
Start with a capital letter, and end with a period.

corn tomato fruit seed

Trace and write these sentences.

Bees leave smelly footprints.

Cicadas are the loudest insects.

Write a sentence using one or more of these words.
Start with a capital letter, and end with a period.

bee   cicada   loud   smelly

Trace and write this sentence that contains every letter in the alphabet.

The quick brown fox jumps over the lazy dog.

Write a sentence using as many letters of the alphabet as you can.

Trace these sentences, and then write them on your own.

Anna is an astronaut.

Alex ate an awesome apple.

Trace these words. Then write a sentence using two or more of the words.

apple art astronaut actor

awake asleep ape arctic

Trace these sentences, and then write them on your own.

Ben plays a banjo in a band.

Bella likes ballet and baseball.

Trace these words. Then write a sentence using two or more of the words.

band   baseball   banjo   ballet

basketball   bat   ball   big

Trace these sentences, and then write them on your own.

Chloe cut a chocolate cake.

Crabs can creep and crawl.

Trace these words. Then write a sentence using two or more of the words.

crab creep crawl cake can

color cat crocodile cute

Trace these sentences, and then write them on your own.

Dave drew a dancing dog.

Did dinosaurs dig ditches?

Trace these words. Then write a sentence using two or more of the words.

dog   dinosaur   ditch   dance

did   dirt   dream   do   did

Practice E

Trace these sentences, and then write them on your own.

Eve exercises each evening.

Use every exit at the end.

Trace these words. Then write a sentence using two or more of the words.

exercise   exit   end   every

each   evening   escape   erupt

Practice **F**

Trace these sentences, and then write them on your own.

Flames flickered from the fire.

Fred flew over a football field.

Trace these words. Then write a sentence using two or more of the words.

flame fire flicker fly flew

football field fun from

Trace these sentences, and then write them on your own.

Guinea pigs graze green grass.

Grace gave a ghost a gift.

Trace these words. Then write a sentence using two or more of the words.

green   give   gave   ghost   goal

good   go   get   gross   gold

Practice **H**

Trace these sentences, and then write them on your own.

Have you hiked a high hill?

Henry has a happy hedgehog.

Trace these words. Then write a sentence using two or more of the words.

high   have   happy   hill   hippo

hide   home   horse   hope

Trace these sentences, and then write them on your own.

I imagine I am an ice skater.

I see an interesting insect.

Trace these words. Then write a sentence using two or more of the words.

I in ice imagine insect into

idea ill is ivy itch if

Trace these sentences, and then write them on your own.

Joe wore jeans and a jacket.

Julia just joined a judo class.

Trace these words. Then write a sentence using two or more of the words.

just   judo   jacket   jeans   jump

joy   join   jet   jail   job   jewel

Trace these sentences, and then write them on your own.

The knight knew a kind king.

Katie's kitten is on her knee.

Trace these words. Then write a sentence using two or more of the words.

kitten keep karate keen kind

kid kitchen know key

Trace these sentences, and then write them on your own.

Lambs love to leap over logs.

I like Little Leo, the lazy lion.

Trace these words. Then write a sentence using two or more of the words.

like love little lion lemon

lazy live leg lift last lollipop

Trace these sentences, and then write them on your own.

My mother met a mermaid.

Matt likes movies and music.

Trace these words. Then write a sentence using two or more of the words.

music   movies   meet   milk

mouse   most   my   mother

Trace these sentences, and then write them on your own.

Noah is now a nimble ninja.

Nanette's nickname is Nan.

Trace these words. Then write a sentence using two or more of the words.

name ninja now new none

no nuts nasty need

Practice O

Trace these sentences, and then write them on your own.

Otto the octopus is orange.

On is the opposite of off.

Trace these words. Then write a sentence using two or more of the words.

on off of orange octopus

out over owl own ox old

Trace these sentences, and then write them on your own.

Pepper is a playful puppy.

Pete painted his purple pumpkin.

Trace these words. Then write a sentence using two or more of the words.

play puppy pumpkin paint

pink person pig paw

Trace these sentences, and then write them on your own.

The queen gave a quick quiz.

Quinn qualified for the quest.

Trace these words. Then write a sentence using two or more of the words.

quiet   quick   quiz   quarter

queen   quit   question   quack

Trace these sentences, and then write them on your own.

Ruby rode in a red rocket.

Rob read about rare reptiles.

Trace these words. Then write a sentence using two or more of the words.

rocket   read   reptile   rare

run   ride   race   rhino

Trace these sentences, and then write them on your own.

Susie swam in the salty sea.

James saw six scaly snakes.

Trace these words. Then write a sentence using two or more of the words.

fish   sailor   sea   sand   ship

sun   shell   surf   storm   shark

Trace these sentences, and then write them on your own.

The triplets put up a tent.

Tom tried out table tennis.

Trace these words. Then write a sentence using two or more of the words.

tent tennis table try talk

taxi truck to test train tree

Trace these sentences, and then write them on your own.

A unicorn uses an umbrella.

The unjust umpire upset us.

Trace these words. Then write a sentence using two or more of the words.

use   unicorn   umpire   under

UFO   up   usual   universe   us

Practice V

Trace these sentences, and then write them on your own.

Vivian drives a violet van.

Victor Vee is the village vet.

Trace these words. Then write a sentence using two or more of the words.

vet village violet van violin

vase very vulture vast

74

Trace these sentences, and then write them on your own.

Who went walking with Will?

Which wand was Willow's?

Trace these words. Then write a sentence using two or more of the words.

wing   who   which   water   win

was   with   wish   whale

Trace these sentences, and then write them on your own.

Xavier took a taxi to Texas.

Next Max will explore Mexico.

Trace these words. Then write a sentence using two or more of the words.

next fox taxi X-ray box

extra mix fix relax six

Trace these sentences, and then write them on your own.

Have you seen a yellow yak?

Yasmine yearns for a yo-yo.

Trace these words. Then write a sentence using two or more of the words.

yo-yo years you yak yarn

yellow yoga young yolk

Practice Z

Trace these sentences, and then write them on your own.

Zach's zoo has zero zebras.

Zoe draws six zany zigzags.

Trace these words. Then write a sentence using two or more of the words.

zoo   zip   zero   zany   zone

zap   zigzag   zest   zoom   zinc

All About Me

Write your full name here.

Write your address here.

Write your phone number here.

You can copy this page for further practice on your own.